Teaching Notes

Contents

An Old Red Hat

Mr Fox's Socks

No Problem!

The Mouse with No Name

Little Mouse Deer and the Crocodile

The Tortoise and the Baboon

Introduction

The *Snapdragons* series is a rich mix of different kinds of stories presented as picture books with expertly written text carefully levelled to provide reading practice at each stage in Key Stage 1.

This set of six books at Stage 4 concentrates on developing the early reading skills that children need to become competent readers. It includes six stories told in patterned language with a predictable structure. These stories introduce children to early key words as well as useful vocabulary, such as numbers and colour words, relating to the different contexts.

The books at Stage 4 include stories based in familiar settings which reflect everyday life and the readers will quickly identify with the family members, school friends and pets, and recognise their experiences. There are also animal fantasy tales and traditional stories from other cultures.

The books at Stage 4 increase in length and will help children to build up stamina in their reading. Children are encouraged to look at the illustrations for visual cues to the words in the text, and to find out what is happening in the story. The picture book presentation will also encourage children to tell the story in their own words so that they develop their oral skills.

How to introduce the books

Before reading the story for guided or independent reading, always read the title and talk about the picture on the cover.

Go through the book together, looking at the pictures and talking about them. If there are context words (listed in the chart on page 4) that are new or unfamiliar, point them out and read them with the children. Read the story to the children, encouraging confident children to join in with you.

This booklet provides prompts and suggestions for using the books in groups and for guided, group and independent activities, matched to text, sentence and word level objectives. There are also separate Guided Reading Cards available for six titles at each stage.

Suggestions are also provided for speaking and listening activities, writing activities, and cross-curricular links. You can use these suggestions to follow on from your reading or at another time.

Reading notes are also provided in each book. They can be found on the inside front and back covers of each book. These suggest friendly prompts and activities for parents or carers reading with their children at home.

Reading skills

Stage 4 develops:
- confidence with longer texts
- the ability to sustain a story from one book to another
- the ability to understand more complex plots within a book
- the ability to be more reflective about reading
- strategies for checking that reading makes sense
- growing confidence in writing independently.

Vocabulary chart

Stage 4		
An Old Red Hat	Year 1 High Frequency Words	an back boy girl got had have home man new not off old saw there what with one two three red
	Context words	bus market nest pennies
Mr Fox's Socks	Year 1 High Frequency Words	about down good got had have his home little made night not one put saw some that them these three took two when who will your
	Context words	box Fox Grandma hole mice socks
No Problem!	Year 1 High Frequency Words	about back but do don't help him home many new not now one people take that then there too were what your green red blue
	Context words	assistant jacket like looked problem shop
The Mouse with No Name	Year 1 High Frequency Words	back but came could door down has her little name new now off one or out ran school then there these took tree very were will with green white five
	Context words	bird blew chased children mouse wind
Little Mouse Deer and the Crocodile	Year 1 High Frequency Words	as by could did first help him how jump(ed) last little made make many next not now off one saw so then there three too two us want when will one to ten
	Context words	crocodile deer hungry mouse river side
The Tortoise and the Baboon	Year 1 High Frequency Words	again back first from had his house last made more must off once so time too took way when your
	Context words	baboon dinner eaten hands laugh(ed) mud(dy) tortoise wash(ed)

Curriculum coverage chart

Stage 4	Speaking and listening	Reading	Writing
An Old Red Hat			
NLS/SLL	T9/Y1T2 5	T4, S7, W2	T14
Scotland	Level A	Level A	Level A
N. Ireland	Activities: b, c, e, g Outcomes: a, b, c, d, e	Activities: a, b, c Outcomes: b, c, d, e, f	Outcomes: b, c, f, h
Wales	Range: 1, 3, 5 Skills: 1, 2, 3	Range: 1, 2, 4, 5, 6 Skills: 1, 2	Range: 1, 2, 3, 6, 7 Skills: 1, 2, 3, 7, 8, 9
Mr Fox's Socks			
NLS/SLL	T8/Y1T2 5, 8	T7, S3, W2, W3	T15
Scotland	Level A	Level A	Level A
N. Ireland	Activities: b, c, e, g Outcomes: a, b, c, d, e	Activities: a, c Outcomes: b, c, d, e, f	Outcomes: a, b, f, h
Wales	Range: 1, 3, 5 Skills: 1, 2, 3, 4, 5, 6	Range: 1, 2, 4, 5, 6 Skills: 1, 2	Range: 1, 2, 3, 6, 7 Skills: 1, 2, 3, 7, 8, 9
No Problem!			
NLS/SLL	Y1T2 7	T4, T7, S1, W10	T14
Scotland	Level A	Level A	Level A
N. Ireland	Activities: a, f, g Outcomes: a, b, c, d, e	Activities: a, b, c, e Outcomes: b, c, d, e, f	Outcomes: b, c, f, h
Wales	Range: 1, 3, 5 Skills: 1, 2, 3, 4, 5, 6	Range: 1, 2, 4, 5, 6 Skills: 1, 2	Range: 1, 2, 3, 6, 7 Skills: 1, 2, 3, 7, 8, 9
The Mouse with No Name			
NLS/SLL	T9/Y1T2 8	T4, S3, W3	T14, T15
Scotland	Level A	Level A	Level A
N. Ireland	Activities: b, c Outcomes: b, d	Activities: a, b, c, e Outcomes: b, c, d, e, f	Outcomes: a, b, f, h
Wales	Range: 1, 2, 5 Skills: 1, 2, 3	Range: 1, 2, 4, 5, 6 Skills: 1, 2	Range: 1, 2, 3, 6, 7 Skills: 1, 2, 3, 7, 8, 9
Little Mouse Deer and the Crocodile			
NLS/SLL	Y1T2 7	T8, S6, W7	T15
Scotland	Level A	Level A	Level A
N. Ireland	Activities: a, g Outcomes: a, b, c, d, e	Activities: a, b, e Outcomes: b, c, d, e, f	Outcomes: a, b, c, f, h
Wales	Range: 1, 3 Skills: 1, 2, 3	Range: 1, 2, 4, 5, 6 Skills: 1, 2	Range: 1, 2, 3, 6, 7 Skills: 1, 2, 3, 7, 8, 9
The Tortoise and the Baboon			
NLS/SLL	T9/Y1T2 8	T5, S1, W7	T14
Scotland	Level A	Level A	Level A
N. Ireland	Activities: b, c, g Outcomes: b, c, d	Activities: b, c Outcomes: b, c, d	Outcomes: b, f, h
Wales	Range: 1, 5 Skills: 1, 2, 3	Range: 1, 2, 4, 5, 6 Skills: 1, 2	Range: 1, 2, 3, 6, 7 Skills: 1, 2, 3, 7, 8, 9

An Old Red Hat

Reading the story

Introducing the story

- Look at the front cover and read the title. Ask the children: *What is the picture on the cover? Who do you think this hat belongs to?*
- Look through the pages, and talk about the setting.
- Ask the children to find the word "market", and find an illustration that shows the market.

During reading

- Praise the children when they read the words in speech marks with an expressive tone, and the number words with confidence.
- Prompt the children to use the picture clues to work out new and unfamiliar words.
- Ask the children to find the question marks as they read.

Observing Check that the children:
- use both text and illustrations to make sense of what they read
- recognise where speech marks are used to denote dialogue.

Group and independent reading activities

Text level work

Range from another culture/predictable and patterned language

Objective To re-tell stories, giving the main points in sequence and to notice differences between written and spoken forms in re-telling, e.g. by comparing oral versions with the written text; to refer to relevant phrases and sentences (T4).

You will need word cards from the story:
nest, bus, lady, man, girl, home
- Ask the children to work with a partner and share a set of word cards.
- Ask them to find the words in the text, and to put them in the order they occur in the story.

- Ask them to use the words, and their order, to re-tell the story to each other.

Observing Do the children match the words on the cards with the words in the text?

Sentence level work

Objective To use capital letters for names and for the start of a sentence (S7).
You will need the following sentences written without capital letters:
ada had a nest.
"that's not a nest!" said mum.
a boy on the bus saw ada.

- Ask the children to re-write the sentences and put capital letters in the correct places.
- Ask them to swap their sentences with a friend and read the sentences carefully.

Observing Do the children recognise two uses of capital letters in the sentences, i.e. for the beginning of the sentence and for names? Do they read each other's sentences carefully?

Word level work

Objective To investigate, read and spell words ending in "ll" (W2).
You will need pens and whiteboards, alphabet strips or alphabet frieze.
- Ask the children to find a word in the text that tells them what Ada wanted to do with the eggs. (p5 sell them).
- Write "sell" on the board and erase the initial letter. Ask the children to suggest other letters that could replace the "s", and to write the words on their boards.
- Collect all the children's suggestions and ask them to practise spelling them using Look, Cover, Write and Check.

Observing Do some of the children suggest consonant clusters to begin the word, e.g. smell, spell?

Speaking and listening activities

Objectives To become aware of character and dialogue, e.g. by role-playing parts when reading aloud stories or plays with others (T9); To re-tell stories, ordering events using story language (Y1T2 5).

- Ask some of the children to take the roles of Ada or Ada's mother.
- Ask them to sit in the hot-seat and describe what they did in the story.
- Ask the other children to question them, using words such as "why" and "how".

◀▶ **Cross-curricular link**
Numeracy: solve simple problems involving money (e.g. *Ada sold 3 eggs for 3 pennies. How much does one egg cost? How much would 4, 5 and 6 eggs cost?*)

Writing

Objectives To represent outlines of story plots using, e.g. captions, pictures, arrows to record main incidents in order (T14).

- Discuss where the story took place. (at home, on a bus and at the market)
- Demonstrate how to draw a circular flow-chart on the board, beginning and ending at home, and adding the other locations to the circle to make a story map.
- Ask the children to draw their own flow-chart and to write a sentence or caption about each place on their story map.

Mr Fox's Socks

Reading the story

Introducing the story

- Look at the front cover and read the title. Ask the children to look at the illustration and to say what Mr Fox is holding. Ask the children to find the word "Socks" in the title.
- Ask the children to look through the text at the illustrations and find out what the story is about.
- Point out any new or difficult words to the children, e.g. p3 "night", p13 "dream".

During reading

- Praise the children when they follow the text with their eyes, self-correcting as they read.
- Prompt the children to use the pictures and initial sounds to help them read the interest words.
- On page 3, ask: *Where is the punctuation that shows when someone is speaking?* Ask them to point to the first and last speech mark and read the words in between. Repeat this on other pages where there is speech.

Observing Check that the children:
- read the dialogue with an expressive tone
- include the words in speech bubbles as they read.

Group and independent reading activities

Text level work

Range fantasy/predictable and patterned language

Objective To discuss reasons for, or causes of, incidents in stories (T7).
- Ask the children to turn to page 3. Ask: *Why did Grandma make socks for Mr Fox?*
- On page 12, ask: *Why did Mr Fox put the mice outside?*

- On page 14, ask: *Why did Mr Fox say "Oh dear!"?*
- On page 15, ask: *Why doesn't Mr Fox need socks?*

Observing   Are the children able to describe the reasons for the events?

Sentence level work

Objective   To predict words from preceding words in sentences and investigate the sorts of words that "fit", suggesting appropriate alternatives, i.e. that make sense (S3).

You will need the following sentences written on strips of card or paper:

> Grandma had _____ Mr Fox some socks.
> Then he _____ his tea.
> Mr Fox saw a _____ in his socks.
> "I do not _____ these black socks."

- Ask the children to read the sentences and to write a word in the gap that makes sense.
- Ask the children to look through the story, find the sentences and compare their versions with the text. Ask: *Do they still make sense?*

Observing   Do the children read the whole sentence before suggesting words to fill the gap? Do their choices "fit" the sentences?

Word level work

Objectives   To investigate, read and spell words ending in *ck* (W2); To discriminate, read and spell words with initial consonant clusters, e.g. *bl, cr, tr, str* – Appendix list 3 (W3).

- Write the words "fox" and "socks" on the board. Explain that they rhyme but have different spellings.
- Ask the children to suggest other words that rhyme, and write some of their suggestions under the word with the same spelling pattern, e.g.

fox	socks
box	locks
	clocks
	frocks

- Ask the children to add words to the list. Provide a list of suitable consonant clusters and blends to help those who need it, e.g. "bl", "st", "cr", "sh", "ch".

Observing Do the children experiment with different beginnings, saying them aloud to see if they make sense?

Speaking and listening activities

Objectives To identify and discuss characters, e.g. appearance, behaviour, qualities; to speculate about how they might behave (T8); To re-tell stories, ordering events using story language (Y1T2 5); To act out own and well known stories, using different voices for characters (Y1T2 8).

- Choose children to take the role of the mice from the story.
- Ask them to sit in the hot-seat and describe what they do in the story.
- Ask the other children to question them about why they did things, and how they felt at different times in the story.
- On page 16, model how to read Mr Fox's words with expression, emphasising the word 'And' beginning the second sentence.

◀▶ **Cross-curricular link**
PSHE: living things have needs

Writing

Objective To build simple profiles of characters from stories read, describing characteristics, appearances, behaviour with pictures, single words, captions, words and sentences from text (T15).

- Ask the children to draw a picture of Mr Fox, and to use both the text and illustrations to write words or captions around the picture, describing Mr Fox's appearance and character.

No Problem!

Reading the story

Introducing the story

- Look at the front cover and read the title. Discuss the illustration with the children and ask them to suggest what the story might be about.
- Look through the pages, talking about what happens in the illustrations. Ask the children to suggest what problems there are in the story.
- Identify any new or difficult words in the text, e.g. p2 "bought", p6 "friend", "bored", p10 "assistant", p15 "people".
- Ask the children to return to the front cover and find the word "Problem".

During reading

- Praise the children when they follow the text with their eyes, only finger-pointing when they have difficulty.
- On page 3, ask the children: *What didn't Sami like about the new jacket?* Point to the word "green".
- On page 8, ask: *Why are these words written in large, bold print?* Encourage them to read the words in an expressive tone.
- On pages 12 and 13, ask the children to read the speech bubbles and say who speaks these words.

Observing Check that the children:
- read the colour words on sight
- self-correct, using a range of strategies
- understand why Sami changes his mind about the green jacket.

Group and independent reading activities

Text level work

Range familiar setting/colour words/predictable and patterned language

Objectives To re-tell stories, giving main points in sequence and to notice differences between written and spoken forms in re-telling (T4); To discuss reasons for, or causes of, incidents in stories (T7).

- Ask the children to take turns to sit in the hot-seat as Sami and to re-tell the story using their own words.
- Ask the other children to ask Sami questions about what happened, using "Why" to begin their questions.
- Encourage the children to use "because" in their answers.

Observing Do the children understand that each event has a cause?

Sentence level work

Objective To expect reading to make sense and check if it does not, and to read aloud using expression appropriate to the grammar of the text (S1).

You will need the following sentences written on strips, or on the board:

> Dad bought Sami a new jacket.
> Dad and Sami went to town.
> Sami was bored.
> Dad was not there.
> Sami and the shop assistant looked for Dad.

- Ask the children to work with a partner.
- Give each pair of children two sets of muddled sentence strips.
- Ask the children to read the sentences to each other and discuss the order they should be in to make sense.
- Ask them to read their chosen order to each other.

Observing Do any children put the sentence "Dad bought Sami a new jacket" at the end of the series?

Word level work

Objectives To learn new words from reading and shared experiences and to make collections of personal interest or significant words and words linked to particular topics (W10).

- Ask the children to look through the story and write down the colour words in the text.
- Ask them add other colours they can see in the illustrations.
- Ask them to read their lists of colours and note how they are spelt, as you write them on the board.
- Ask the children to practise spelling the words using Look, Cover, Write and Check.

Observing Do the children attempt to spell the colours in the illustrations?

Speaking and listening activities

Objective To take turns to speak, listen to others' suggestions and talk about what they are going to do (Y1T2 7).

- Discuss why Sami lost his Dad in the shop.
- Ask the children what Sami did that was sensible. (He asked the assistant for help.)
- Ask the children to say what they would do if they got lost while shopping, e.g. who to ask for help.

◀▶ **Cross-curricular link**
PSHE: people who help us/asking for help

Writing

Objective To represent outlines of story plots using, e.g. captions, picture, arrows to record main incidents in order (T14).

- Discuss the main events of the story with the children and scribe their ideas (no more than six) on the board.
- Ask the children to draw a story map of the incidents, using arrows to link the main incidents and writing a sentence for each incident.

The Mouse with No Name

Reading the story

Introducing the story

- Look at the front cover and read the title. Ask the children to find the words "Mouse" and "Name" in the title.
- Look through the pages together, focusing on the illustrations.
- Identify any unfamiliar words with the children, e.g. p9 "chased", p10 "playground", p15 "flew".

During reading

- Praise the children when they follow the text with their eyes, only finger-pointing when they have difficulty.
- On page 2, ask the children to show you where the sentences end.
- On page 6, ask: *Why does Miss Green drop the mouse?*
- On pages 8, 16 and 17 ensure the children read the text in the right direction.
- Encourage the children to read the spoken words with expression.

Observing Check that the children:
- read the high frequency words on sight
- use the term "sentence" and identify the full stops
- recognise who speaks the words in speech bubbles?

Group and independent reading activities

Text level work

Range familiar setting/predictable and patterned language

Objective To re-tell stories, giving the main points in sequence and to notice differences between written and spoken forms in re-telling, e.g. by comparing oral versions with the written text; to refer to relevant phrases and sentences (T4).

- Ask children to imagine they are the "mouse with no name" and to take turns to sit in the hot-seat with the story book.

- Ask them to describe what happens in the story using "I", as if they were the mouse.
- Encourage other children to ask questions about how the mouse felt and what it thought.
- Ask the child in the hot-seat to find the relevant page in order to help them answer the questions.

Observing Do the children recall the events? Do they scan the book for relevant pages?

Sentence level work

Objective To predict words from preceding words in sentences and investigate the sorts of words that "fit"', suggesting appropriate alternatives (S3).
You will need the following incomplete sentences written on strips:

Then the wind _____ and Miss Green _____ the mouse.
The mouse _____ up a tree.
"The cat will _____ it!" the children _____.
The children _____ back into the classroom.

- Read the sentences to the children, and ask: *What sorts of words are missing?* (action words/verbs)
- Ask the children to suggest words that make sense of the sentences, and write them in the gaps.
- Ask the children to find the sentences in the book, and compare their choices with the text.

Observing Do the children recall verbs used in the story or suggest others from their own experience, e.g. "The cat will *eat* it" the children *cried*.

Word level work

Objective To discriminate, read and spell words with initial consonant clusters, e.g. *bl, cr, tr, str,* – Appendix list 3 (W3).

- Write the initial clusters, "bl", "fl", "dr", "tr", and "gr" on the board.
- Ask the children to look through the text and find a word that begins with each cluster. ("blew", "flew", "dropped", "tree", "Green")

- Ask them to write the words and practise their spelling using Look, Cover, Write and Check.
- Some children may be able to scan the text for other words with initial consonant clusters. ("playground", "classroom")

Observing Do the children find the words quickly and easily, scanning the lines of text?

Speaking and listening activities

Objectives To become aware of character and dialogue, e.g. by role-playing parts when reading aloud stories or plays with others (T9); To act out well-known stories, using different voices for characters (Y1T2 8).

- Provide the children with stick-puppets of the characters and ask groups to act out the story.

◀▶ **Cross-curricular link**
PSHE: to realise that people and other living things have needs, and that they have responsibilities to meet them

Writing

Objectives To represent outlines of story plots using, e.g. captions, pictures, arrows to record main incidents in order, e.g. to make a class book, wall story, own version (T14); To build simple profiles of characters from stories read, describing characteristics, appearances, behaviour with pictures, single words, captions, words and sentences from text (T15).

- Discuss the appearance of the mouse in the illustration on page 5. Ask the children to suggest how the mouse feels, e.g. sad, lonely.
- Model how to draw a mouse and write a word describing it (e.g. sad), then an arrow to another mouse picture. Add a word to describe it (e.g. scared/frightened).
- Ask the children to draw their own series of mice with a word or phrase describing how it feels in the story, and link them with arrows to show the order of the story.

Little Mouse Deer and the Crocodile

Reading the story

Introducing the story

- Look at the front cover and read the title. Explain that the Little Mouse Deer comes from Southeast Asia.
- Look through the pages, talking about what happens in the illustrations and discussing the jungle setting.
- Ask the children to turn to page 4 and find the word "crocodile".

During reading

- Prompt the children to use the illustrations to help them work out words when they have difficulty.
- Encourage the children to use the punctuation to help them make sense of the text, re-reading where a sentence runs on to more than one line.
- On pages 18 and 19, ask the children to point to the number words as they read them.

Observing Check that the children:
- use more than one strategy to make sense of what they read
- read familiar key words with confidence.

Group and independent reading activities

Text level work

Range fantasy/from another culture/predictable and patterned language/numbers

Objective To identify and discuss characters, e.g. appearance, behaviour, qualities; to speculate about how they might behave; to discuss how they are described in the text; and to compare characters from different stories or plays (T8).

- Ask the children to find a word in the text that describes the crocodile's character. (p23 "foolish")
- Ask the children: *What words could describe Little Mouse Deer's character?* List their suggestions on the board.
- Ask the children if they have read any other stories with a clever character using a trick to escape, e.g. "Anansi", "The Gingerbread Man", "Brer Rabbit", "The Three Billy Goats Gruff".
- Ask them to write a sentence describing Little Mouse Deer.

Observing Do the children think of other words with the same meaning as foolish, e.g. silly, stupid?

Sentence level work

Objective To use the term "sentence" appropriately to identify sentences in text, i.e. those demarcated by capital letters and full stops (S6).

- Ask the children to turn to page 2 and find the start and end of the sentence.
- Ask them to read the text on page 3. Ask: *How many sentences are there?* (two)
- Ask the children to turn to page 8 and read the text. Ask: *How many sentences are there?* (three)
- Ask the children to look through the rest of the book and find any other pages where there are three sentences. (p 15)

Observing Do the children look for capital letters and full stops to identify complete sentences?

Word level work

Objective To recognise the critical features of words, e.g. common spelling patterns (W7).
You will need pens and whiteboards

- Ask the children to point to the word "Deer" on the cover and emphasise the long "ee" sound.
- Ask them to turn to page 3 and find another word with the same sound and spelling. ("see")

- Ask the children to read the word "leaves" and emphasise the vowel sound.
- Write "ee" and "ea" on the board as headings. Ask the children to look through the text to find any words with the same spelling patterns and write them under each heading. ("Deer", "see", "three", "leaves", "eat")

Observing Do the children scan the pages to find the spellings?

Speaking and listening activities

Objective To take turns to speak, listen to others' suggestions and talk about what they are going to do (Y1T2 7).

- Ask the children about Mouse Deer's name, and discuss how it is two other animal names.
- Ask them to suggest other strange animals they could invent by joining two other names together, e.g. Crocodile Frog.
- Ask them to describe what their invented animal looks like.

◀▶ **Cross-curricular link**
Numeracy: numbers to 10

Writing

Objective To build simple profiles of characters from stories read, describing characteristics, appearances, behaviour with pictures, single words, captions, words and sentences from the text (T15).

- Ask the children to suggest words that describe Little Mouse Deer's character and behaviour in the story. Write their suggestions on the board.
- Ask the children to look at the illustrations in the story and suggest words that describe Little Mouse Deer's appearance. Add their suggestions to the board.
- Ask the children to draw Little Mouse Deer and add captions to describe his appearance.
- Ask them to finish by writing a sentence about Little Mouse Deer's character.

The Tortoise and the Baboon
Reading the story

Introducing the story

- Look at the front cover and read the title. Ask the children to point to the word "Tortoise" and "Baboon".
- Ask the children to look quickly through the book at the illustrations. Ask the children: *Where do you think the story takes place?*
- Identify any new or difficult vocabulary, e.g. p6 "angry", "hungry".

During reading

- Praise the children when they follow the text with their eyes, only finger-pointing when they have difficulty.
- Prompt the children to use the pictures to help them understand the story, e.g. on pages 4 and 7, ask: *What is Tortoise thinking about*?
- On page 12, ask: *Why do Baboon's hands keep getting dirty?*

Observing   Check that the children:
  - ■ use more than one strategy to help them work out words
  - ■ recognise thought bubbles.

Group and independent reading activities

Text level work

Range   fantasy/traditional story/from another culture/predictable and patterned language

Objective   To identify and record some key features of story language from a range of stories, and to practise reading and using them, e.g. in oral re-tellings (T5).

- Ask the children to turn to page 4 and read the sentence to them, emphasising the words "he was hot, he was tired and he was hungry". Ask them to look through the text and find where these words appear again. (p13)

- Ask the children to work with a partner and take turns to tell the story to each other, using the illustrations as a prompt.
- Ask the children to say what was different about each other's version of the story and to check them against the text in the book.

Observing Do the children use the language of the story in their re-tellings, e.g. words to link events ("When", "so").

Sentence level work

Objective To expect reading to make sense and check if it does not, and to read aloud using expression appropriate to the grammar of the text (S1).

You will need a selection of sentences from the story written on word cards, e.g.

Baboon was hot, he was tired and he was hungry.

So Baboon set off across the mud and washed his hands again.

- Give each child a muddled-sentence and ask them to put the words into an order that makes sense.
- Ask the children to read their sentence aloud, and then to check it against the text.

Observing Do the children take account of capital letters and punctuation when ordering the words?

Word level work

Objectives To recognise the critical features of words, e.g. length, common spelling patterns (W7).

You will need white boards and pens

- Turn to page 3 and ask the children to find the word that describes how Tortoise walks. ("slowly")
- Write the word on board and ask the children to repeat it aloud. Point out the ending letter "y".
- Ask the children to look through the rest of the text and write other words with the same ending. (hungry, angry, muddy, dirty)

Observing Do the children notice that all the words describe something?

Speaking and listening activities

Objectives To become aware of character and dialogue, e.g. by role-playing parts when reading aloud stories or plays with others (T9); To act out own and well-known stories, using different voices for characters (Y1T2 8).
You will need stick puppets or masks of Tortoise and Baboon

- Ask the children to work with a partner and ask each to take the role of one character.
- Ask them to act out the story in their own words and to imitate how the animals move.
- Encourage the children to add to the dialogue, and to use expressive voices and actions.

◀▶ **Cross-curricular link**
PHSE: recognising what is fair and unfair; maintaining personal hygiene

Writing

Objective To represent outlines of story plots using, e.g. captions, pictures, arrows to record main incidents in order, e.g. to make a class book, wall story, own version (T14).

- Look together through the illustrations and discuss the places in the story. (where Baboon and Tortoise meet, Baboon's house, Tortoise's house, the path, the river)
- Ask the children to draw a map of the story and label each place.

Oxford Reading Tree resources at this level

There is a range of material available at a similar level to these stories which can be used for consolidation or extension.

Stage 4

Teacher support
- Teacher's Handbook
- Flopover Book
- Big Book for Stage 4 Stories
- Guided Reading Cards for Stage 4 Stories
- Take-Home Card for each story
- Extended Stories
- Storytapes / More Storytapes
- Context Cards
- Workbooks 4a and 4b
- Woodpeckers Introductory Phonic Workbooks C and D
- Sequencing Cards Photocopy Masters
- Group Activity Sheets Book 2 Stages 4–5
- ORT Games Stages 4 and 5

Further reading
- Oxford Reading Tree Storybooks for Core Reading
- Stage 4 Playscripts
- Stage 4 Spaarows and More Sparrows (for consolidation)
- Fireflies Non-Fiction
- Fact Finders Units A and B
- Glow-worms Poetry

Electronic
- Clip Art
- Stage 4 Talking Stories
- ORT Online www.OxfordReadingTree.com
- Floppy and Friends

For developing phonics
- Alphabet frieze, Tabletop Alphabet Mats, Alphabet Photocopy Masters
- Card Games
- First Story Rhymes

OXFORD
UNIVERSITY PRESS

Great Clarendon Street, Oxford OX2 6DP

Oxford University Press is a department of the University of Oxford. It furthers the University's objective of excellence in research, scholarship, and education by publishing worldwide in

Oxford   New York

Auckland   Cape Town   Dar es Salaam   Hong Kong   Karachi Kuala Lumpur   Madrid   Melbourne   Mexico City   Nairobi   New Delhi   Shanghai   Taipei   Toronto

With offices in

Argentina   Austria   Brazil   Chile   Czech Republic   France Greece   Guatemala   Hungary   Italy   Japan   Poland   Portugal SingaporeSouth Korea   Switzerland   Thailand   Turkey   Ukraine Vietnam

Oxford is a registered trade mark of Oxford University Press in the UK and in certain other countries

British Library Cataloguing in Publication Data

Data available

Cover illustrations by Sanja Rescek

Teacher's Notes: ISBN 978 0 19 845534 9

10 9 8 7

Page make-up by Fakenham Photosetting, Fakenham, Norfolk

Printed in China by Imago